THE COCKTAIL PROGRAM
FOR YOUR BAR AT HOME

# POUR HOUSE

BY ALLEN MASK

*RAISE YOUR BAR*

Pour House © 2025 Allen Mask
Published by Camp Digital
Identity by Lion Lion Studio
Layout by Yue Li Art

ISBN (Paperback): 979-8-9930917-0-9
ISBN (Hardback): 979-8-9930917-1-6
ISBN (E-book): 979-8-9930917-2-3

**Enjoy responsibly.**

This book is intended for use by adults of legal drinking age in their respective jurisdictions. The recipes, techniques, and suggestions contained herein are for informational and entertainment purposes only.

Alcoholic beverages should be consumed in moderation. Please be mindful of your own limits and the safety of yourself and others. Do not drink and drive. The author and publisher shall have no liability for any damages, losses, or injuries that may occur as a result of the information or recipes provided in this book, including but not limited to, excessive consumption or misuse of alcohol or other ingredients.

Always ensure you are aware of and comply with all applicable local, state, and national laws regarding the purchase, possession, and consumption of alcoholic beverages. If you have concerns about alcohol consumption, please consult a healthcare professional.

"One of the finest things in life is the hospitality of a host who really cares."

—Fred Rogers

## WHAT IF . . .

What if the best bar in town was your kitchen table?
What if that 5-star local watering hole was your sister's garage?
What if your barber made a better martini than your bartender?

Getting "smart about drink" will change the way you think about hospitality. You don't have to be a "mixologist" to make someone a cocktail they love. Creating a beverage program for your home (or apartment) is really about developing a new set of tools for making your guests feel seen and your people feel loved.

Raiseyour.bar (the website) is a simple pool of resources for anyone curious about cocktail culture. It's all-things hobby mixology for the passionate and professional. Beyond this book, there are podcasts, articles, videos, downloads, and more, all of which are designed to inspire the creativity of a host.

Pour House was designed to be a quick flip; intentionally sparse and void of superfluous details and explanations. I spent a lot of time developing this system and even more time learning to explain it in as few words as possible. Like my favorite recipes, the ideas presented here are short, sweet, and simple.

# RAISE YOUR BAR

## PREFACE

In 2015, during a season of life I fondly remember as "Silicon Valley, the Musical," a few friends and I agreed to an experiment: see how much money we could save if we insourced the whole drinks-after-work thing.

We were in the grind of our careers, fighting the sale of our souls to the bottomless pit of internet culture and software empire-building. Just a few misplaced southerners undercover as tech bros in San Francisco, drinking way too much of our monthly budgets at iconic bars like Trick Dog, Smuggler's Cove, and ABV.

It was a glorious time, actually. The meals we didn't eat at work were enjoyed in Michelin-grade test kitchens on any block of the city. The drinks we didn't have at the office were often at legendary pop-ups manned by award-winning bartenders. We spent weekdays on the Peninsula and weekends in Sonoma, all of which inspired us to do more cooking and cocktailing of our own.

I spent the next 10 years distilling everything I was learning into a running note, the gist of which is presented here in Pour House, a layman's field guide for building a bar at home. Pour House is a short blend of my favorite tips, tricks, and frameworks sure to inspire your next cocktail. It's one of the marquee resources of raiseyour.bar, a little website I made with friends for friends.

Pour House is designed to be more illustrative than exhaustive. I'm an enthusiast, not an expert, after all. So please take my suggestions with a salted rim :)

And remember—don't forget to read your Surgeon General's Warning. This project isn't meant to glorify drinking in excess. Alcohol is toxic. But as they say: The poison is in the dosage.

Cheers!

# Table of Contents

# FOUNDATIONS

# Composition
# Beer & Wine
# Cocktails
# Glass
# Ice
# Garnish

# COMPOSITION

A full bar generally consists of beer, wine, and the materials and ingredients suited for making mixed drinks. The team at Raise Your Bar is mostly focused on cocktails. But first, a moment for our good friends, beer and wine.

# BEER & WINE

Any unpretentious employee at your favorite vineyard or craft brewery can learn you up on the lore of hops and grapes. But it's a deep scene, the navigation of which might require recruiting friends far more specialized than I am.

But in my experience with beer and wine, it's best to offer something "lighter," like a Pilsner or a Kölsch, and something "heavier," like an Amber or an IPA. This chart is surely an oversimplification, but I wish I had something like it when I was getting started.

Goes without saying that you should have soft drinks for those that are dry or designated to drive. This can be anything from flat water to sparkling cider. We'll leave that to you, but try to keep it interesting! The goal is to make our friends in recovery or seasons of temperance feel just as catered to as everyone else.

# Beer   Wine

## LIGHTER

Blonde
Kölsch
Lager
Pilsner
Saison
Wheat

## LIGHTER

### WHITE
Albariño
Sancerre

### SKIN CONTACT
Rosé

### RED
Gamay
Pinot Noir

### SPARKLING
Cava

## HEAVIER

Amber
Barleywine
Double
IPA
Porter
Stout

## HEAVIER

### WHITE
Chardonnay
Viognier

### SKIN CONTACT
Orange

### RED
Syrah
Zinfandel

### SPARKLING
Champagne

# COCKTAILS

# cock·tail

/ˈkäkˌtāl/

noun

1.  an alcoholic drink consisting of a spirit or several spirits mixed with other ingredients, such as fruit juice, lemonade, or cream.

A good cocktail is a balanced cocktail. That's why good boulevardiers can taste like cranberry juice. And good daiquiris can taste like limeade.

You want each and every ingredient working together to blend in rather than stand out. Pull any lever you can to keep that one drink from tasting too much like that one thing.

## Boozy ◆◆◆◆◆◆◆◆◆◆◆◆

## Dry ◆◆◆◆◆◆◆◆◆◆◆◆◆

## Bitter ◆◆◆◆◆◆◆◆◆◆◆◆

And don't be afraid to get spicy or savory, should your guest (or the occasion) allow. The best bartenders will tell you cocktails are equal parts art and science, so don't be afraid to get creative.

One of my favorite things to do when I'm working on a well-known drink is to order it out a few times to better understand its range. Studying with and learning from your favorite hosts will tighten your technique and refine your taste.

## Juicy

## Sweet

## Sour

## GOOD COCKTAILS ARE JUDGED BY FOUR THINGS:

◆ Recipe

◆ Glass

◆ Ice

◆ Garnish

I was taught to judge a cocktail in four parts: recipe, glass, ice, and garnish. Recipes address the "how much of what?" question, but remember, just like in math, you can have the right formula and still get the wrong answer.

You're right that a great drink is more than the sum of its parts, but nailing a recipe will only solve 25% of the equation. Once you have a solid formula, it's time to think about something equally important but often forgotten: presentation.

Excellent presentation is critical for the successful enjoyment of a cocktail. In my experience, people remember the drinks that were as easy on the eyes as they were going down. My wife is famous for thinking prettier drinks taste better. And you know what, I hate to admit it, but she's right.

That said, don't feel the need to break your bank when you're practicing behind closed doors. Our guests who love to test my in-progress creations know anything that I'm "working on" will surely fall short of its eventual packaging. I think it's totally fine to save your time and money when you're not hosting or making what I call "production" or "menu-ready" cocktails.

# GLASS

When I say glass, I'm referring to whatever vessel is assigned to host your beverage. And it doesn't have to be glass, by the way. Anything from grandma's crystal to your beer pong cups are fair game.

Drinks served "down" are generally presented over ice and seated in something short like a lowball or old fashioned glass. Drinks that are traditionally presented without ice are (most often) served "up" in something like a v-shaped martini or a "Nick & Nora" glass (Google it for a fun backstory).

Your higher volume cocktails usually come "tall" as they almost always include lengthening agents like juice or soda. And "neat" drinks are to be enjoyed as-is at room temp in anything from a shot glass to a brown bag (for those of us still bottle-fed).

Lowball  or  Coffee mug

# Down

Coupe  or  Wine glass

# Up

Highball  or  Pint glass

# Tall

Snifter  or  Shot glass

# Neat

# ICE

Ice is, well, ice! Frozen water, they say. The cocktail class can wax poetic about the sins and sanctities of ice programs and varieties, but at the end of the day, ice should be thought of as a mechanism for simultaneous chilling and diluting.

There is an entire cottage industry around selling people all sorts of molds and components for rendering ice that's clear and/or in novel shapes. These can be fun, and I use several myself, but don't let them distract you. Just make sure you have ice, any kind of ice, and plenty of it. As long as you have what you need to shake, stir, and serve, you're good.

Pebbles or Boats

# Small

Blocks or Spheres

# Large

# GARNISH

The garnish is a good drink's finishing touch; a visual and olfactory aid in the discernment and enjoyment of your beverage. Garnishes can be anything from modest wheels to magnificent peels, depending on your desired balance of form and function.

I used to think garnishes were a waste of time, at least within the context of a home bar. Aren't we just making drinks for friends? And shouldn't said drinks be judged more by how they taste than how they look? But it turns out garnishes actually play a huge role in previewing, communicating, and confirming the notes and flavors of your cocktail. And your investment in getting them right will, at the very least, further showcase the thought and care you've put into creating a memorable experience for your guest(s).

Citrus pressed shell   or   Hand expressed shell        Freeze-dried or Fresh

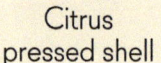

## Hull                              Wheel

Strip or Shape

## Peel

Metal or Wood

## Pick

 or

Single
(edible flower)      Multiple
(handful of basil)

## Herbs

# METHODS

# Tools
# Techniques

# TOOLS

If you're anything like me, it won't be hard to immediately waste your drinking budget on all sorts of obscure cocktail-making tools. But what's that old saying? If you know better, you do better? Here is a short list of starting points for tools of the trade, and visit raiseyour.bar for access to our preferred set of brands as well as instructional videos with best practices.

The most important takeaway for this section? Don't wait to get started. Even access to a modestly equipped kitchen will provide you with most of what you need to make a lot of the cocktails in this book (even if you're substituting household items for professional bar tools). As Arthur Ashe once said, "Start where you are, use what you have, do what you can."

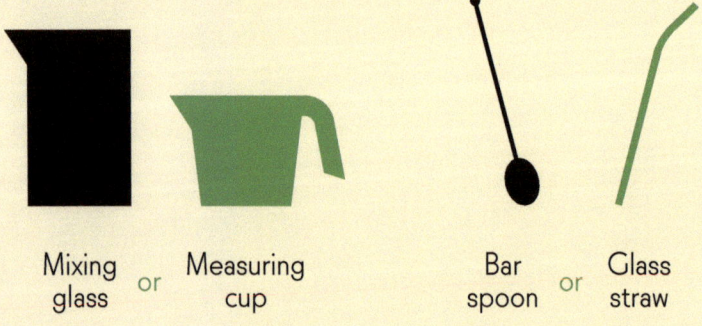

| Mixing glass | or | Measuring cup | | Bar spoon | or | Glass straw |

## Stirring

Julep strainer   or   Slotted spoon

Hawthorne strainer   or   Small mesh strainer

# Straining

Boston shaker   or   Mason jar

# Shaking

Paring knife   or   Pocket knife

Citrus peel   or   Steak knife

# Garnishing

# TECHNIQUES

Some drinks you swizzle, some drinks you dry shake, some drinks you roll, but at the end of the day, the two basic methods for merging or multiplying ingredients are stirring and shaking. The good news is that most of you will know where to start with both.

Stirring and shaking are equal parts chilling, mixing, and diluting. They're not the only techniques, but I'd like to think they're the most important. Raiseyour.bar can teach you about all sorts of other advanced techniques to impress your friends, but try to keep it simple until you have the confidence and consistency to try something new.

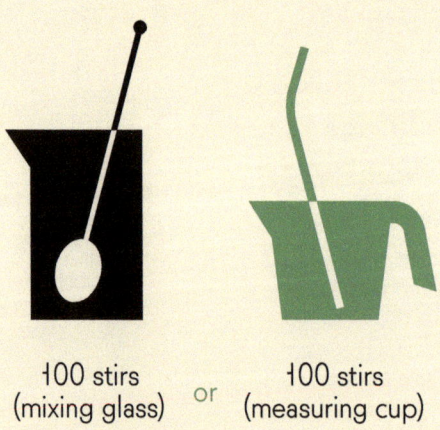

100 stirs      or      100 stirs
(mixing glass)         (measuring cup)

## Stirring

Pummel to press the oils, juices, sugars, and spices out of fruits, vegetables, and herbs

# Muddling

 or

Shake until frosty (boston shaker)

Shake until frosty (mason jar)

# Shaking

# INGREDIENTS

It doesn't take long for a good bar's ingredients list to move from manageable to overwhelming. Presented here is what I would think of as the "minimum viable" bottle shop and grocery store shopping list to fully power the cocktail corner of your bar.

This list is not exhaustive, yet has been meticulously curated to not only support the menus in the back of the book, but to give you a strong toolkit with which you can make infinitely more drinks than we've shared. But be careful, it's easy to get carried away! I personally have a rule that I don't keep anything on my bar that doesn't work hard in at least three drinks I love.

You'll notice I don't provide references to specific bottles (visit raiseyour.bar for guidance on brands). This book is designed to introduce you to the ideas behind the great drinks, rather than prescribe my preferences for their preparation. Fight the urge to distract yourself with questions like "Which rum?" or "Does it have to be bourbon?" We'll get to that later.

INGREDIENTS

# Spirits

Brandy

Gin

Rum

Vodka

Whiskey

# Vermouths

Bianco Vermouth (White)

Sweet Vermouth (Red)

# Fruits/
Herbs

Brandied Cherries

Jalapeño

Lemon

Lime

Mint

Orange

# Mixers

Club Soda

Coconut Water

Grapefruit Juice

Tonic Water

# Liqueurs

Orange

# Amaro/ Other

Aperitivo

Red Bitter

Vanilla Extract

# Syrups

Cream of Coconut

Orgeat

Raw Agave Nectar

Raw Sugar (See Recipe)

Rich Honey (See Recipe)

Rock Candy (See Recipe)

# Bitters

Cocktail

Orange

# SYRUPS

Rock Candy

Raw Sugar

Rich Honey

Once upon a time, I maintained 14 house-made syrups until I was reminded that only a few really matter. They say simple is when there's nothing left to take away, rather than nothing left to add. Most drinks on the menus in Pour House can be made with some combination (or product adjacent to) a simple sugar syrup.

Don't get me wrong, it's great to have options, but try to avoid creating a "paradox of choice." Whether you prefer store-bought or made from scratch, always make sure you're stocked with what's essential before you take up space with what's nice to have. And once you can make them in your sleep, feel free to get a bit sporty and make them your own.

# ROCK CANDY

Rich and simple syrup.

# 2 parts superfine sugar

# 1 part water

1. Combine ingredients
2. Blend (at room temperature)
3. Cover and refrigerate

# RAW SUGAR

Rich and robust syrup, with flair.

# 2 parts raw sugar

# 1 part water

# Dash(es) of vanilla, to taste

# Pinch(es) of salt, to taste

1. Combine ingredients
2. Blend (at room temperature)
3. Cover and refrigerate

# RICH HONEY

Rich honey syrup.

# 2 parts honey
# 1 part water

1. Simmer water
2. Combine ingredients
3. Stir
4. Cover and refrigerate

# MENUS

## Classics

Old Fashioned
Manhattan
Martini
Negroni
Sidecar

## Standards

Soda
Tonic
Spritz
Juice
Spirit

## Favorites

Flatiron
Gold Rush
Spicy Margarita
Mezcal Daisy
Southside

## Tiki

Rum Punch
Mai Tai
Junglebird
Piña Colada
Navy Grog

Pour House presents four distinct menus that include the "who's who" of cocktails. Said another way, I believe these are the 20 drinks you want in your back pocket.

The idea to organize the drinks into nested menus was inspired by Tradition, one of my favorite prohibition-era, speakeasy-style bars in San Francisco. Tradition, at least at the time of this writing, is closed. But I'll never forget my first time flipping through page after page of cocktails organized by the eras.

The interpretations of these drinks are manifold, which is why each recipe features approachable "starting measures" that make for a smart (but safe) default recipe. Over time, you'll make these your own, but learning all 20 as-written might save you years of trial and error.

**MENUS**

# CLASSICS

If you only learn five cocktails, learn these. Seriously. Classics are the building blocks for so many of your favorite drinks. They're the Mount Rushmore of cocktail culture, and for good reason.

- Old Fashioned
- Manhattan
- Martini
- Negroni
- Sidecar

# OLD FASHIONED

Cocktail, first of its name. These were to Don Draper what P.F. Flyers were to Benny the Jet.

# 2 oz whiskey

(something cask strength, preferably rye)

# 1/4 oz
# raw sugar syrup

# 1 dash
# cocktail bitters

# 1 dash
# orange bitters

| | |
|---|---|
| **TOOLS** | Mixing glass, bar spoon, julep strainer |
| **TECHNIQUE** | Stirred with ice |
| **GLASS** | Lowball |
| **ICE** | Big cube |
| **GARNISH** | Orange peel |

# MANHATTAN

To the city, with love, from West Egg. A kiss of this will surely get you back in the New York groove.

# 2 oz whiskey

(for an alt on the traditional rye, try an overproof bourbon)

# 1 oz
# sweet vermouth

# 2 dashes
# orange bitters

# 1 bar spoon
# brandied cherry syrup

| | |
|---|---|
| **TOOLS** | Mixing glass, bar spoon, julep strainer |
| **TECHNIQUE** | Stirred with ice |
| **GLASS** | Coupe |
| **ICE** | Served without ice |
| **GARNISH** | Brandied cherry |

CLASSICS

# MARTINI

There are many ways to martini, but this is my favorite.
Try "3:1" with a Plymouth-style gin and a bright, bianco vermouth.

# 3 oz gin

(something earthy with mild notes of juniper)

# 1 oz
# bianco vermouth

| | |
|---|---|
| **TOOLS** | Mixing glass, bar spoon, julep strainer |
| **TECHNIQUE** | Stirred with ice |
| **GLASS** | Coupe |
| **ICE** | Served without ice |
| **GARNISH** | Lemon twist |

# NEGRONI

We might not agree on three ingredients; we might not agree on equal measures; but one thing we CAN agree on: It's Negroni Week somewhere.

# 1 oz gin

# 1 oz sweet vermouth

# 1 oz red bitter

| | |
|---|---|
| **TOOLS** | Mixing glass, bar spoon, julep strainer |
| **TECHNIQUE** | Stirred with ice |
| **GLASS** | Lowball |
| **ICE** | Big cube |
| **GARNISH** | Orange peel |

# SIDECAR

You ride shotgun; I'll drink sidecar. May this timeless sour remind you of why the sailors say "Brandy, you're a fine girl. What a good wife you would be."

# 2 oz brandy

(e.g., cognac)

# $1/2$ oz lemon

# $1/2$ oz orange liqueur

# $1/4$ oz raw sugar syrup

| | |
|---|---|
| **TOOLS** | Boston shaker, Hawthorne strainer |
| **TECHNIQUE** | Shaken with ice |
| **GLASS** | Coupe |
| **ICE** | Served without ice |
| **GARNISH** | Orange peel |

# STANDARDS

Raiseyour.bar talks a lot about "Standards," or popular styles of frequently ordered drinks. What's standard about them is that each implies a template that's easy to remember and riff on.

- ◆ Soda
- ◆ Tonic
- ◆ Spritz
- ◆ Juice
- ◆ Spirit

# SODA

Whether in-flight or on-float, you'll always know
what to expect from a simple spirit and soda.
They're easy to drink and hard to make wrong.

# 1 1/2 oz spirit
(e.g., blanco tequila)

# 4 - 6 oz soda

| | |
|---|---|
| **TOOLS** | Bar spoon |
| **TECHNIQUE** | Stirred in glass |
| **GLASS** | Highball |
| **ICE** | Rocks |
| **GARNISH** | Citrus twist (e.g., lime) |

# TONIC

Like a soda, touched for the very first time.
Like a soda, with citrus, sugar, and quinine.

# 1 1/2 oz spirit

(e.g., floral gin)

# 1/4 oz citrus

(e.g., lime)

# 4 - 6 oz tonic

| | |
|---|---|
| **TOOLS** | Bar spoon |
| **TECHNIQUE** | Stirred in glass |
| **GLASS** | Highball |
| **ICE** | Rocks |
| **GARNISH** | Citrus twist (e.g., lime) |

# SPRITZ

A good spritz is a refreshing blend of bubbles and botanicals. Make it in the glass, and make it your own! The variations are infinite.

# 4 oz bubbles

(e.g., pét-nat)

# 2 oz amaro, vermouth or bitter

(e.g., red aperitivo)

# 1 1/2 oz club soda

| | |
|---|---|
| **TOOLS** | Bar spoon |
| **TECHNIQUE** | Stirred in glass |
| **GLASS** | Wine |
| **ICE** | Rocks |
| **GARNISH** | Citrus wedge (e.g., orange) |

# JUICEBOX

These never disappoint. Especially if you're working with premium ingredients. Adding a "Juicebox" to your menu is an easy way to give your bar some seasonal flair.

# 3 oz
# cold-pressed juice

(e.g., pineapple, watermelon, etc.)

# 1 oz spirit

(e.g., vodka, tequila, etc.)

| | |
|---|---|
| **TOOLS** | Bar spoon |
| **TECHNIQUE** | Stirred in glass |
| **GLASS** | Highball |
| **ICE** | Rocks |
| **GARNISH** | Citrus twist (e.g., lime) |

# SPIRIT

Certain brands don't mix well, and we love them just the same. Whether you're ordering something simple or sipping something sacred, let your spirit take a solo. Rocks, or not.

# 3 oz spirit

(something high on your shelf, like long-aged scotch)

**GLASS**     Lowball

# FAVORITES

There are a handful of drinks that, in my experience, are always top of mind for somebody. But maybe they're inescapable for a reason? There's almost certainly an audience for one of these bad boys.

- Flatiron
- Gold Rush
- Spicy Margarita
- Mezcal Daisy
- Southside

# FLATIRON

This is the martini I make for people that don't know a martini is a martini. It's as sophisticated, but more approachable.

# 1 1/2 oz vodka
(something premium)

# 1 1/2 oz bianco vermouth

# 1/4 oz orange liqueur

| | |
|---|---|
| **TOOLS** | Mixing glass, bar spoon, julep strainer |
| **TECHNIQUE** | Stirred with ice |
| **GLASS** | Coupe |
| **ICE** | Served without ice |
| **GARNISH** | Lemon twist |

# GOLD RUSH

Trading picks and shovels for sh*ts and giggles,
the "Gold Rush" is basically a "Bee's Knees,"
if it identified as a whiskey sour.

# 2 oz whiskey

(e.g., corn whiskey)

# 3/4 oz
# rich honey syrup

# 1/2 oz lemon

| | |
|---|---|
| **TOOLS** | Boston shaker, Hawthorne strainer |
| **TECHNIQUE** | Shaken with ice |
| **GLASS** | Lowball |
| **ICE** | Rocks |
| **GARNISH** | Lemon wheel |

# SPICY MARGARITA

Made "Tommy's Way," so just lime, agave and tequila, but spicy. Just remember: not all jalapeños are created equal!

# 2 oz tequila

## 1/2 oz
## raw agave syrup

## 1/2 oz lime

## muddled
## jalapeño coins

## pinch of salt

| | |
|---|---|
| **TOOLS** | Boston shaker, Hawthorne strainer, mesh strainer, muddler |
| **TECHNIQUE** | Shaken with ice and double strained |
| **GLASS** | Lowball |
| **ICE** | Rocks |
| **GARNISH** | Lime hull |

# MEZCAL DAISY

A daisy is your simple sour with a boost of fizz. I tend to skip the soda, but this smoky, margarita-like riff goes down easy. Fitting, since "margarita" literally means "daisy."

# 2 oz mezcal

# 1/2 oz orange liqueur

# 1/2 oz lemon

# 1 bar spoon rock candy syrup

| | |
|---|---|
| **TOOLS** | Boston shaker, Hawthorne strainer |
| **TECHNIQUE** | Shaken with ice |
| **GLASS** | Coupe |
| **ICE** | Served without ice |
| **GARNISH** | Lemon wheel |

# SOUTHSIDE

Gimlets, anyone? Try a Southside, its slightly more bitter, slightly more herbaceous cousin. It's different, but familiar.

# 2 oz gin

## 1/2 oz rock candy syrup

## 1/2 oz lime

## 1 dash orange bitters

## Muddled mint

| | |
|---|---|
| **TOOLS** | Boston shaker, Hawthorne strainer, mesh strainer |
| **TECHNIQUE** | Shaken with ice and double strained |
| **GLASS** | Coupe |
| **ICE** | Served without ice |
| **GARNISH** | Mint leaf |

# TIKI

Tiki is more than a style of drink—it's a way of life. Who can resist the allure of escapism? Southern California's exotic brand of Polynesian Pop gave us a canon of cocktails that sound, seem, and taste immortal.

- Rum Punch
- Mai Tai
- Junglebird
- Piña Colada
- Navy Grog

# RUM PUNCH

"Punch" is most likely a loanword from Hindi, where "pāñch," meaning "five," refers to the typical number of ingredients in a large-format Caribbean sour. Remember it with this rhyme: one sour, two sweet, three strong, four weak—plus a little spice to make it nice.

# 2 oz black tea

# 1 1/2 oz rum

(something overproof)

# 1 oz
# raw sugar syrup

# 1/2 oz lemon

# 2 dashes
# cocktail bitters

| | |
|---|---|
| **TOOLS** | Boston shaker, Hawthorne strainer |
| **TECHNIQUE** | Shaken with ice |
| **GLASS** | Lowball |
| **ICE** | Rocks |
| **GARNISH** | Lemon wheel |

# MAI TAI

While its origin story is contested, this stalwart riff on the daiquiri is always en vogue.

# 2 oz rum
(preferably a blend of rums)

# 1/2 oz lime

# 1/2 oz orgeat

# 1/4 oz
# raw sugar syrup

# 1 bar spoon
# orange liqueur

| | |
|---|---|
| **TOOLS** | Boston shaker, Hawthorne strainer |
| **TECHNIQUE** | Shaken with ice |
| **GLASS** | Lowball |
| **ICE** | Rocks |
| **GARNISH** | Lime hull |

# JUNGLE BIRD

Birds of a feather drink together. This tiki sour is slightly less sweet, but good to the bitter end.

# 1 1/2 oz rum

(something dark and moody, like black rum)

# 1 1/2 oz pineapple juice

# 3/4 oz red bitter

# 1/2 oz lime

# 1/2 oz raw sugar syrup

| | |
|---|---|
| **TOOLS** | Boston shaker, Hawthorne strainer |
| **TECHNIQUE** | Shaken with ice |
| **GLASS** | Lowball |
| **ICE** | Rocks |
| **GARNISH** | Orange wheel |

# PIÑA COLADA

"If you like making love at midnight, in the dunes
on the cape. You're the lady I've looked for.
Come with me and escape."

# 2 oz rum
(something overproof)

# 1 1/2 oz pineapple

# 1 1/2 oz
# cream of coconut

# 1 dash
# cocktail bitters

| | |
|---|---|
| **TOOLS** | Boston shaker, Hawthorne strainer |
| **TECHNIQUE** | Shaken with ice |
| **GLASS** | Lowball |
| **ICE** | Rocks |
| **GARNISH** | Brandied cherry |

# NAVY GROG

With 18th-century roots in the British Royal Navy's daily rum ration, this Tiki classic is a delightful change of pace from your standard rum sour.

# 3 oz rum

(preferably a blend of rums)

# 1 oz
# rich honey syrup

# 1 oz grapefruit

# 1/2 oz lime

| | |
|---|---|
| **TOOLS** | Boston shaker, Hawthorne strainer |
| **TECHNIQUE** | Shaken with ice |
| **GLASS** | Lowball |
| **ICE** | Rocks |
| **GARNISH** | Lime hull |

## AFTERWORD

Hear that bell? Class dismissed! Hopefully this material isn't leaving you with more questions than answers. Or, if it is, maybe that's a good thing?

Building a bar is like that old cliché: the journey is more important than the destination. Have fun, experiment, be creative, and most important: be a host. I often mention at raiseyour.bar that these efforts to educate hobby bartenders and nerdy drinkers are about upgrading your hospitality, not increasing your consumption.

When I first started taking the notes that became this book, I was doing so to inform a letter to my sons for their 21st birthdays.

I found myself sharing drafts with so many friends and colleagues that I decided to publish, if anything to make sharing easier. It was also my last chance to write a short book before artificial intelligence starts writing everything for us :)

Visit raiseyour.bar for more resources like Pour House, and subscribe to our mailing list for in-home cocktail tips, tricks, and recipes.

We appreciate your support!

Allen Mask
Raise Your Bar

## RESOURCES

I could easily write an entirely separate book on my favorite resources for all-things-cocktails. Those that know me well will remember their frequent chuckles at the fact that I take my backpack everywhere, and that the only thing guaranteed to be in my backpack is some kind of book about making drinks.

Pour House (this book) truly is a small piece of the larger movement that is Raise Your Bar. Raiseyour.bar is a pool of inspiration for unpretentious millennial bon vivants that love to host people in their homes.

I don't reference raiseyour.bar here as a cop out, or as a shameless act of self-promotion (though both can be true). I've just spent so much time thinking through and documenting my personal canon of resources that I only ever notice what's missing vs. what's included.

Check out raiseyour.bar when you can, and consider this "resources" section as a digital menu of everything else we've produced for your enjoyment and continued education.

## THANK YOU

To Carlton, for smiling through (and fighting the urge to spit out) my many botched drinks. And, to our (for now) little boys who always pretend to shake with me when someone orders a sour. I look forward to the day they're old enough to make MY drinks :)

To Finn, Miche, Will, Witty, Sayed, and Plandrew for being among my original sources of inspiration. From our first cocktails to our first home menus, there is no Pour House without you!

To Jacob and Julia for the brand, and Yue for the layout. It's all just copy without art. And because Raise Your Bar is a movement, not just a series of "products," the brand (and its many manifestations) might be the most important piece of the larger project.

To Deirdre and Collin, my siblings, and authors, for paving the way. The success of your books have inspired me beyond measure.

To all of my editors and readers (you know who you are) for the years of critique. I'll admit this has taken way too long but I'm hopeful that, with your help, we got it right.

I'd be remiss to suggest that the many contributors to Pour House could ever be thanked on less than 200 (let alone two) pages. I'm so grateful for the scores of friends, mentors, neighbors, and colleagues that have helped me refine this program over the years. I have deeply appreciated everyone's encouragement (and patience).

Surely this short book is just a first step on the journey of building community around your home bar. Please be on the lookout for future follow-ups and updates.

## ABOUT THE AUTHOR

Allen Mask is an investor, operator, and entrepreneur, best known for his work as a freelance creative, management consultant and executive coach.

Mask discovered his love for cocktails as a bar back at a small restaurant in college, and later expanded and refined his palate as a mixology influencer traveling the world. Mask's first book is Pour House, a layman's field guide for building a bar at home.

# CONVERSIONS

| US Measure | Metric | Notes |
| --- | --- | --- |
| Drop | ~0.05 mL | |
| Dash of bitters | ~0.9 mL | |
| 1 bar spoon | 5 mL | |
| 1 tsp | 5 mL | |
| 0.25 oz | 7.5 mL | splash |
| 0.33 oz | 10 mL | rounded from 9.8 mL |
| 1 Tbsp | 15 mL | |
| 0.5 oz | 15 mL | half jigger |
| 0.75 oz | 22 mL | |
| 1 oz | 30 mL | 1 jigger |
| 1.25 oz | 37 mL | |
| 1.5 oz | 45 mL | standard pour |
| 2 oz | 60 mL | |
| 2.5 oz | 75 mL | |
| 3 oz | 90 mL | often stirred cocktail |
| 4 oz | 120 mL | tall builds |
| 6 oz | 180 mL | |

## Quick Rules of Thumb

1 tsp = 5 mL

1 Tbsp = 15 mL

1/2 oz = 15 mL

1 oz = 30 mL

Round to nearest 5 mL when converting

www.ingramcontent.com/pod-product-compliance
Lightning Source LLC
Chambersburg PA
CBHW040904120626
46551CB00006B/634